ANANTA

THE INFINITE JOURNEY OF MAA KALI

BY PRAGATI MUKHERJEE

RIDHZWORLD PUBLISHING

First Printing Edition @ 2026

Paperback ISBN: 978-81-999105-3-9

eBook ISBN: 978-81-999105-0-8

Printed & published by

Ridhzworld Publishing,

Hadapsar, Pune, India

https://www.ridhzworld.com

Table of Contents

Part I - Meeting the Dark Mother

Chapter 1

MEETING MAA KALI: THE DARK MOTHER

The first time many of us encounter Maa Kali is not through scripture, but through an image. Perhaps it is a framed picture on a wall, a temple murti lit by flickering diyas, or a pandal during Kali Puja, where drums beat and the air is thick with incense. Her tongue is outstretched, her hair wild and unbound, her garland strung with severed heads. To an unfamiliar eye, this sight can feel startling, even frightening. And yet, in the very same moment, her devotees fold their hands, whisper "Maa," and feel a rush of safety, love, and recognition.

It is in this paradox that Maa Kali reveals herself. She is at once terrifying and tender, fierce and comforting. She is the one who stands on the edge of the cremation ground and also the one who holds her children close in times of fear. To those who look only at the surface, she may seem like a goddess of darkness and destruction. To those who know her, she is the Dark Mother, whose very darkness is a promise that nothing within us, no fear, no pain, no secret is too ugly to be held, transformed, and freed.

In the vast landscape of Hindu thought, Maa Kali stands as one of the most profoundly significant forms of the divine feminine. While her form may seem fearsome at first glance, to her bhaktas she is Maa, a mother who nurtures and protects. Her very name carries layers of meaning. Derived from Sanskrit roots, "Kali" is commonly understood as "the dark one" or as "time" (kaal), pointing to her as the relentless devourer of ego, of illusion, and of all that must end. She is worshipped as Adya Shakti, the original power, the beginning of all things, the primal creative force and the eternal feminine.

Maa Kali's presence is not limited to one era or one text. Mentions of her can be traced across the Puranas and other sacred writings, reaching as far back as at least the fourth century CE. Over time, she emerges not only as a fearsome goddess of battle, but as a deeply symbolic and spiritual figure whose stories carry meaning for both the outer world and the inner life of a seeker.

One of the most important texts in which she appears is the Devi Mahatmya, a section of the Markandeya Purana that has shaped Shakta traditions for centuries. Composed of around 700 verses, it presents the Devi as an omnipotent yet compassionate mother who restores balance whenever adharma threatens the cosmos and the human heart. Within this sacred text, Maa Kali emerges at a climactic moment in the battle against the demon brothers Shumbha and Nishumbha, where all the scattered rays of Shakti—gentle, protective, fierce, all-knowing, converge into a single blazing presence.

Over centuries, she has become a powerful symbol of femininity, not in a narrow sense, but as Shakti, the female principle of creative energy that pervades all existence. In her, we find a femininity that is not confined to softness alone. She is uncompromising power and bottomless compassion, fierce protection and deep tenderness. Whether in temples, in village shrines, in tantric practice, or in the quiet bhakti of a household altar, she continues to embody the truth that the divine feminine can be both the storm and the shelter.

To truly engage with Maa Kali is to accept that we may not be able to understand her completely. She is, by nature, boundless. Yet we can begin to approach her through her stories, her symbols, her names, and the countless ways she is loved and feared across traditions. The journey starts with acknowledging that behind the garland of skulls, the sword, the darkness of her skin, and the intensity of her gaze, stands a mother who refuses to abandon her children, no matter how turbulent the times.

This book is an invitation to walk a little closer to her. To see how Maa Kali appears in scripture and story, in folk villages and cremation grounds, in devotional songs and in the struggles of modern life. To meet her not only as a terrifying destroyer, but as a mother who cuts away what harms us, so that what is true and whole can finally breathe.

In the chapters that follow, we will move from the grand cosmic narratives of the Devi Mahatmya to the details of her form and symbols, to tales of her grace and fury, and then to the living traditions and contemporary resonances through which Maa Kali continues to shape hearts, communities, and inner worlds. For now, it is enough to stand before her and say, perhaps a little hesitantly, perhaps with deep familiarity: "Maa, help me see you as you are, and help me see myself through your eyes."

Chapter 2

THE GLORY OF THE GODDESS: DEVI MAHATMYA

On certain evenings in many parts of India, especially during Navratri or special pujas, the air in temples and homes changes. Lamps are lit, bells ring softly, and a priest or elder opens a sacred book. As the first verses of the Devi Mahatmya are recited, the sound seems to thicken the space, ancient Sanskrit syllables rolling like waves, carrying with them the weight of centuries. Even if one does not understand every word, something in the rhythm, the fervour, and the devotion tells us that this is no ordinary text.

The Devi Mahatmya, which literally means "the glory of the goddess," is one of the most important scriptures of the Shakta tradition. It forms a section of the Markandeya Purana and is composed of around 700 verses that together create a complete vision of the Devi. In these verses, the goddess appears in many forms: gentle and nurturing, fierce and unstoppable, serene and terrifying, yet always completely aware and compassionate. For countless devotees, this text has become a central way of understanding who the Devi is and how she moves through the universe.

According to the Purana, the stories of the Devi Mahatmya are narrated by the sage Medhas to a king who had lost his kingdom and a merchant who had lost his peace of mind. Both were in deep distress, confused by the reversals of life and searching for meaning. They come to the forest, seeking wisdom, and it is there that Medhas tells them the stories of the goddess. In this way, the Devi Mahatmya is not a cold, distant theology. It is offered as medicine to those who are wounded, a mirror for people who have been shaken by loss and uncertainty.

The tales that follow show the goddess as the one who restores order when the balance of the universe is disturbed. Asuras and danavas are powerful beings representing unchecked ambition, cruelty, and adharma who rise again and again to seize control of the three worlds. They defeat the gods, capture their weapons, and claim their thrones. In response, the gods, stripped of their power, turn to the Devi. They gather in the Himalayas, on snow-clad slopes under vast skies, and invoke her with hymns that echo through the mountains. From their combined longing and praise, the Devi manifests: radiant, calm, and infinitely powerful.

One of the most striking features of the Devi Mahatmya is the way it moves between outer and inner realities. On the outer level, we see grand battles, demon armies, storms of weapons, and the Devi riding into war. On the inner level, these scenes symbolise the struggles within each human being. The asuras are not just cosmic villains; they are the forces of greed, anger, ego, fear, and ignorance that disturb our own inner equilibrium. The Devi, in turn, stands for light, clarity, and wisdom; the power that shows us the truth and leads us away from the darkness we create for ourselves.

In this framework, Maa Kali's appearance in the Devi Mahatmya gains even deeper meaning. She emerges during the fierce battle against the demon brothers Shumbha and Nishumbha, at a moment when arrogance and domination seem to reign unchecked. All the gods have been defeated. The universe appears to be under the control of those who believe only in their own power. It is then that the Devi's wrathful, blazing aspect bursts forth. From her own brow arises Maa Kali, a dark, devouring form, the one who laughs in the face of tyranny and cuts through illusion with a single stroke.

For the devotee listening to these verses, perhaps in a dimly lit temple or in a small home shrine, this is not just a story about distant cosmic beings. It is a reminder that whenever injustice seems overwhelming, whenever ego appears to rule unchallenged, whether in the world outside or in the corridors of our own mind, there exists a force that can and will rise to restore balance. Kali's terrifying laughter and unrestrained dance become symbols of a deeper truth: that no false power can last forever, and that kaal, time itself, will eventually devour every form of arrogance.

Over time, the Devi Mahatmya has inspired countless commentaries, translations, and local retellings. In some households, it is recited in full during Durga Puja or Navratri. In others, selected chapters are read in times of crisis, illness, or major change. For many, simply hearing its verses, even without intellectual understanding, brings a sense of comfort and protection as though the Devi is being formally invited to sit in the centre of their lives for a while.

In the Shakta vision, the Devi revealed in the Devi Mahatmya is not just one goddess among many. She is the source from which all forms of the divine feminine arise. Durga, Lakshmi, Saraswati, and Kali are not separate rivals, but different faces of the same boundless Shakti, appearing as needed. To the frightened, she comes as a mother. To the arrogant, she comes as a fierce warrior. To the lost, she comes as a gentle guide. To those ready for transformation, she appears as Kali, who does not hesitate to tear away illusion.

To sit with the Devi Mahatmya, then, is to sit with a scripture that is both mythical and mirror. Its stories of gods, demons, kings and sages do not belong only to some distant age, they echo in our private fears and collective struggles. For anyone who approaches Maa Kali, this text becomes a doorway. It shows us the backdrop against which she appears, the cosmic drama in which her presence becomes necessary, and the kind of world, outer and inner, that she seeks to protect.

As we move from Maa Kali's origin towards understanding the symbolism of her form, it is helpful to remember the atmosphere in which her stories are traditionally told. They are not whispered in secret, nor are they locked away in dusty books. They are sung, chanted, narrated, and re-imagined in homes, temples, and gatherings of devotees. They are living words, meant to be heard with the heart as much as with the mind. In the Devi Mahatmya, the glory of the goddess is not an abstract idea. It is a lived experience of fear turning into trust, of chaos giving way to order, and of darkness becoming a space where the mother's presence can be felt most strongly.

Chapter 3

BORN FROM BATTLE: THE ORIGIN OF MAA KALI

The Devi does not always appear in calm moments of prayer. Sometimes, she arrives in the middle of a storm.

According to the Devi Mahatmya, the origin of Maa Kali is born out of a moment of great crisis. The universe is under siege. Asuras are forces of chaos, greed, and adharma who have risen again, and their power now threatens to overturn the balance of all three worlds. The gods, once radiant and confident, have been driven back. What should have been realms of harmony now echo with fear and unrest.

In this tense atmosphere, the goddess Durga, herself a radiant and powerful form of the Devi, rides into battle. Her lion roars across the battlefield, and her many arms hold weapons granted by the gods. Every movement of hers is precise, purposeful, and filled with an unshakeable resolve. She is the calm centre in the chaos of war and yet, even within that calm, a deeper, more terrifying power waits.

As the battle intensifies, new waves of demonic forces appear. Their cruelty grows, their arrogance deepens. It is in this charged moment that something extraordinary happens. From the furrow of Durga's brow, the space between her eyebrows where concentration and wrath meet, there bursts forth a dark, blazing form. This is Maa Kali.

She emerges not as a gentle, smiling goddess, but as a force that refuses compromise. Her skin is dark, absorbing all light. Her hair flies wild and free. Her tongue is extended and her eyes burn with a fire that sees through every disguise. In her hands she carries weapons, and around her, the very atmosphere shifts. Where Durga holds the balance of restraint and power, Kali is power in its rawest, most unfiltered state.

In this origin, Maa Kali is not separate from Durga; she is Durga's own inner fury and uncompromising clarity made visible. She is the concentrated form of Shakti that arises when the usual limits of patience and gentleness have been crossed. When persuasion has failed, when warnings have been ignored, when adharma has grown bold, it is this aspect of the Devi that steps forward.

On the battlefield, her presence transforms the tide of war. She moves swiftly, cutting down demonic forces that had seemed invincible. Her very laughter shakes the enemy. For those who side with truth and justice, her appearance is a relief, a sign that the universe has not forgotten them. For those who cling to arrogance and cruelty, her sight is a clear message: there is a limit to how far one can go against dharma.

This origin story can be read on many levels. On one level, it is a majestic mythical story about gods and demons, about a divine mother who manifests new forms to protect her children. On another, it speaks to something deeply human. There are times in life when gentle adjustments and small corrections are not enough. There are situations within societies, relationships, or even within our own minds where something more drastic is required. Old patterns, harmful habits, and persistent injustices sometimes need to be faced with Kali-like honesty and finality.

In this sense, Maa Kali's emergence from Durga's brow symbolises a moment of inner awakening. It is the point at which we can no longer tolerate our own self-deception. When the mind, like Durga, has tried every softer method and still finds itself surrounded by inner asuras such as fear, anger, envy, greed, and despair, Kali arises as a fierce determination to cut through them. She is the part of us that says, "Enough," and means it.

The Devi Mahatmya also reminds us that this fierce form is not random anger; it is a force guided by wisdom and compassion. Maa Kali does not destroy for pleasure. She destroys what obstructs harmony, truth, and freedom. Just as a surgeon may remove what is diseased to save the body, Kali removes what is toxic to save the soul. Her violence, as it appears in mythology, is in service of a deeper peace.

In contemporary times, we can see this origin story playing out in quieter ways. A person trapped for years in a harmful situation may one day find the courage to walk away, even if it means facing uncertainty. A community tired of injustice may finally rise and say "no more". An individual struggling with addiction, destructive anger, or long-buried pain may reach a point where transformation is no longer a distant idea but an urgent necessity. In all these moments, something of Kali's energy is present, a fierce love that is willing to end what cannot continue.

Thus, Maa Kali's birth from Durga's brow is not just a dramatic scene from an ancient text. It is a reminder that within the compassionate mother lies a fierce protector, and within us, too, there exists a capacity to call forth clarity and courage when gentler approaches have failed. She shows us that anger, when aligned with truth and guided by conscience, can become a purifying fire rather than a destructive blaze.

As we move forward into understanding her iconography, her garland of skulls, her sword, her severed head, her dark complexion, it is helpful to remember this origin. Every symbol she carries, every aspect of her form, belongs to this same purpose: to free, to protect, and to restore balance, even when the path to that balance passes through destruction. To stand before Maa Kali is to stand before a mother who will comfort us, but who will also, when needed, tear away everything that keeps us from our own truth.

Chapter 4

SYMBOLS OF FIRE AND GRACE: HER FORM AND ICONOGRAPHY

For many devotees, the first meeting with Maa Kali is wordless. It happens in front of an image.

She stands with dark skin, unbound hair, a garland of skulls resting on her chest. Around her waist hangs a belt of severed arms. In one hand she holds a sword, in another a freshly severed head. Her tongue protrudes, her eyes are wide and unblinking, and beneath her feet lies the still body of Shiva. To someone seeing her for the first time, this vision can be overwhelming. Yet for those who love her, every part of this form is a doorway into understanding.

Hindu iconography rarely shows the divine in a simple, neutral way. Every colour, ornament, posture, and object is chosen to teach. Maa Kali is no exception. In fact, her form might be one of the most densely symbolic in the entire pantheon. To read her image is to read an entire philosophy of creation, destruction, time, and liberation.

THE COLOUR OF THE INFINITE

Maa Kali is usually shown with a dark, almost black complexion. At first glance, this darkness may look frightening or mysterious. But in the language of symbolism, black is not only the colour of fear, it is the colour of all the absorbing infinite.

Just as all colours disappear into black, all names and forms dissolve in her. She is the space in which everything appears, and into which everything returns. Her darkness suggests that she is beyond all distinctions of caste, gender, race, and all labels the human mind creates. To stand before her is to stand before that which cannot be easily defined, but within which everything exists.

In a world that often worships fairness, perfection, and surface beauty, Maa Kali's dark form is also a challenge. She refuses to conform to any conventional ideal. Instead, she asks: can you recognise the divine in what you fear or reject? Can you see beauty in the raw, the untamed, and the vast unknown?

THE GARLAND OF HEADS: LETTERS AND LIBERATION

Around her neck hangs a garland of human heads, often described as numbering fifty. At first, this may seem like a purely terrifying ornament. But in the symbolic language of Tantra and Shakta traditions, these heads represent the fifty letters of the Sanskrit alphabet.

Each letter is a unit of sound, and sound is seen as a form of shakti, a creative power. Together, these letters form all possible words, scriptures, mantras, songs, and stories. By wearing them as a garland, Maa Kali is shown as the source and sustainer of all knowledge, speech, and expression. She is the one through whom language arises and into whom it eventually falls silent.

On a more personal level, the garland reminds us that true wisdom is not just accumulated information. It is knowledge that has passed through the fire of experience and surrender. In the presence of Kali, words that are shallow or false tend to fall away. What remains is what is essential, honest, and aligned with truth.

THE BELT OF ARMS: ACTION WITHOUT ATTACHMENT

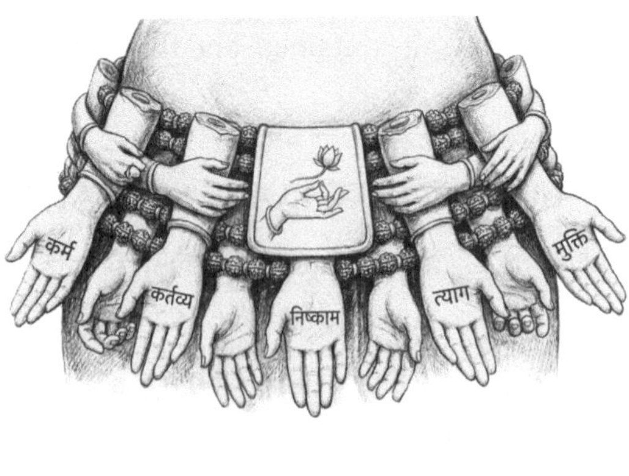

Around her waist, Maa Kali wears a girdle or belt made of severed human arms. Arms are the instruments of action. We use our hands and arms to work, to build, to protect, to grasp, and sometimes to harm. In everyday life, we are deeply attached to the fruits of our actions such as success, recognition, results.

The waistband of arms symbolises karmic action and its consequences. It teaches the principle of performing one's duty fully, yet without clinging to outcomes. The severed arms suggest that the actions we perform, once done, must be let go. We cannot control every result, nor can we carry every burden forever.

Standing before Maa Kali, we are reminded that freedom does not come from withdrawal alone, but from a different way of engaging. Work, love, responsibility, and struggle continue but the grip of "this is mine" slowly loosens. Actions become offerings rather than chains.

THE SWORD AND THE SEVERED HEAD: CUTTING THROUGH ILLUSION

In one hand, Maa Kali holds a sword, in another, she holds a severed human head dripping with blood. These are among her most striking attributes.

The sword represents Viveka, a selective wisdom. It is the sharp clarity that cuts through confusion, denial, and self-deception. In many spiritual traditions, liberation is not achieved by adding more beliefs, but by seeing clearly. Kali's sword is the power of that clear vision. It cuts away what is false, no matter how tightly we cling to it.

The severed head symbolises the ego and the restless intellect. It is not a rejection of intelligence, but a reminder that the mind, when inflated and ungrounded, can become a tyrant. By holding the head in her hand, Maa Kali shows us what happens when ego is surrendered: it is no longer ruling from the top of the body, it has become an offering.

Together, the sword and the head express a powerful teaching: liberation involves the end of false identity. When the ego's grip loosens, what remains is a deeper, quieter awareness that is not constantly threatened. Kali, as the wielder of the sword, becomes the inner force that helps us let go of the stories we tell about who we are, so we can rest in a truth beyond those stories.

THREE EYES: BEYOND PAST, PRESENT, AND FUTURE

Maa Kali is often depicted with three eyes. Her two side eyes see the world of time, the ordinary flow of past, present, and future. Her central eye looks beyond time into the eternal.

In mythic language, her three eyes symbolise her complete awareness of all that has been, all that is, and all that will be. Nothing is hidden from her. She understands not only our actions, but also our intentions, fears, and potential. For the devotee, this is both humbling and comforting. There is no need to pretend before a mother who already sees everything.

In a practical sense, remembering her three eyes can change how we experience our own struggles. When we are trapped in a difficult present, it is easy to believe that this moment is all there is. Kali's gaze reminds us that every experience is part of a much larger unfolding, and that her compassion is not limited to one chapter of our life.

RED AND BLACK: CREATION IN THE HEART OF DISSOLUTION

Alongside her dark complexion, Maa Kali is deeply associated with the colour red. Red is the colour of blood, life force, fertility, and creativity. Often, her tongue is red, her garlands may include red hibiscus flowers, and her surroundings are lit with the warm glow of red and orange lamps.

The combination of black and red in her iconography is not accidental. Black stands for the infinite space in which all things arise and dissolve. Red stands for the dynamic energy that creates, nourishes, and moves all things. Together, they show that in Maa Kali, dissolution and creation are not opposites. They are part of one continuous rhythm.

For us, this means that when something ends under her gaze, a phase of life, a relationship, a habit, a role, it is not merely destruction. In that ending lies the seed of a new beginning. She is present in both the closing of a door, and the quiet opening of another.

THE MOTHER WITHIN THE TERRIFYING FORM

Taken separately, each of these symbols can seem intense. Together, they create an image that has frightened and fascinated devotees for centuries. Yet beneath the skulls, the weapons, and the wild hair, there is a consistent thread: protection and liberation.

Maa Kali's form does not invite easy comfort. She does not promise a life without pain or loss. Instead, she stands as a reminder that the divine is present even in the middle of what we fear most; death, change, endings, and the loss of control. Her iconography asks us to look directly at what we usually avoid, and to discover, in that gaze, a deeper kind of safety.

To meditate on her image is to let her symbols work slowly on the heart. The garland of heads loosens our attachment to empty words. The belt of arms softens our grip on results. The sword invites us to let go of falsehood. The severed head asks us to surrender ego. Her three eyes reassure us that we are seen completely. Her colours hold both the darkness we dread and the life we cherish.

As we move further into Maa Kali's many forms and stories, these symbols will continue to echo in the background and deepen our understanding of her. They remind us that whether she walks through battlefields, village paths, cremation grounds, or the inner landscape of a seeker's heart, she remains the same: a mother who loves fiercely enough to set us free.

Chapter 5

MANY FACES OF MAA: HER FORMS AND DUALITY

Maa Kali does not appear in only one way. Across scriptures, temples, villages, and inner visions, she takes on many forms, each bringing forward a different aspect of her nature. Sometimes she is all-encompassing Mahakali, sometimes the graveyard-dwelling Smashan Kali, sometimes the protective and auspicious Bhadrakali. Together, these forms reveal a goddess who is not limited to a single mood or role, but who moves freely between destruction and creation, terror and tenderness, darkness and compassion.

Through her many names and faces, Maa Kali shows us that the divine feminine is not a flat image. She is a living power that adapts to what is needed, whether it is fierce protection, quiet guidance, deep transformation, or gentle blessing. In knowing her forms, we begin to understand not only who she is, but also the many possibilities within ourselves.

MAHAKALI: SHE WHO HOLDS TIME

Mahakali is often described as the form of Kali who stands beyond time itself. If Kali, as a name, is linked to kaal, the concept of time, then Mahakali is time in its most vast, cosmic sense: the force that devours all beginnings and all endings, while remaining unchanged.

Imagine a devotee standing before an image of Mahakali at the end of a difficult year. So much has changed, relationships, health, work, identity. Plans have dissolved, and new realities have appeared without warning. In the silence of the shrine, the devotee looks up at Mahakali's dark form and feels, perhaps for the first time, that there is a presence which is not swept away by change. She has seen countless lives rise and fall, empires built and broken, stars born and extinguished. Yet she remains, watching, holding, witnessing.

In this form, Maa Kali reminds us that everything in life is marked by time: youth, success, failure, even grief. Nothing we experience is permanent. Mahakali is not asking us to become indifferent; instead, she invites us to loosen our desperate attempts to control the flow of events. When we remember her, we begin to see that while situations come and go, there is a deeper awareness within us that simply witnesses, just like her. In turning to Mahakali, we learn to live fully in each moment, without imagining that any moment can last forever.

SMASHAN KALI: THE TEACHER OF IMPERMANENCE

Among Maa Kali's forms, Smashan Kali is the one who dwells in the cremation ground, the smashan. This is the place most people avoid, where bodies are burned, families grieve, and the finality of death cannot be ignored. It is precisely here that this form of Kali is said to be most present, because the cremation ground strips away all illusions of permanence.

To understand what Smashan Kali teaches, it can help to imagine a simple, human moment.

In a small town by a river, a cremation ground lies just beyond the last line of houses. By day, people hurry past it, eyes lowered. By night, pyres flicker against the darkness, and the air is thick with smoke and whispered mantras. One evening, a young man who has just lost a loved one walks slowly towards this place. The world that once felt solid now seems fragile and unsteady. He sits at a distance from the flames, watching as fire returns a body to ash.

At first, he feels only fear and resistance. Everything in him wants to turn away. But as he continues to sit there, a different sensation arises, a stillness that does not deny the pain, but quietly holds it. In that raw space, he senses a presence that is not sentimental, yet not cruel: an energy that says, “This is the truth, and I am here with you in it.” This is the energy of Smashan Kali.

Smashan Kali does not shield us from the reality of death; she stands exactly where endings happen. Yet, in that very place, she offers a kind of freedom. When we accept that all forms change and pass, our clinging softens. We do not become cold; we become more honest and more compassionate, knowing how precious each moment is. Through Smashan Kali, the cremation ground becomes not only a site of loss, but a place where courage, clarity, and surrender can begin to grow.

BHADRAKALI: THE AUSPICIOUS PROTECTOR

Where Smashan Kali stands at the edge of endings, Bhadrakali appears as a more approachable, protective, and auspicious presence. The word bhadra suggests goodness, welfare, and blessing. In this form, Maa Kali is not less powerful, but her power is felt more as shelter than as storm.

In many homes and temples, Bhadrakali is worshipped as the guardian of the household and community. People come to her with everyday worries like a child’s health, an exam, a financial struggle, a difficult decision. In front of her, the heart speaks freely: “Maa, look after us. Maa, protect us from what we cannot see. Maa, keep harm away from this home.”

We might picture a mother lighting a small diya before Bhadrakali late at night, after everyone else has gone to sleep. The house is quiet. The flame is steady. She folds her hands and whispers the names of each family member, asking for protection and strength. In that soft light, Bhadrakali is not a distant deity of cosmic battles, but a close guardian, as intimate as a mother’s hand resting on a child’s head.

Bhadrakali shows us that divine fierceness is not only about destruction. It is also about fierce care. She protects not by wrapping us in illusions, but by giving us the strength and clarity to face what life brings. Under her gaze, safety does not mean nothing difficult will happen, it means we will not have to face it alone.

ONE GODDESS, MANY MOODS

At first, these forms, Mahakali, Smashan Kali, Bhadrakali might seem very different from one another. One stands beyond time, one in the cremation ground, one at the doorstep of the home. Yet they are all Maa Kali.

Their diversity reflects the complexity of life itself. There are times when we need to remember that everything passes (Mahakali). There are times when we must stare directly at loss and impermanence (Smashan Kali). There are times when we long simply to feel protected and held (Bhadrakali). Maa Kali changes form not because she is inconsistent, but because her compassion is flexible. She meets us where we are.

This apparent contradiction as fierce yet nurturing, destructive yet protective, dark yet compassionate is not a flaw; it is an essential aspect of the divine feminine, the Shakti. She is fierce when protection is required, nurturing when growth is needed, and dark with compassion when dissolution brings peace. Even when the means seem harsh to the unprepared eye, the purpose remains the same: to restore equilibrium and protect what is true and tender.

Through this well-balanced duality, Maa Kali becomes a role model for empowered femininity. She does not apologise for changing forms or for expressing different qualities at different times. She demonstrates that a woman, whether divine or human, need not choose between strength and softness, between warrior and mother, between creative force and restful darkness. In her, all these aspects coexist without conflict.

For readers and devotees alike, her many forms offer permission to be whole. We, too, can protect fiercely when needed and open our hearts gently at other times. We can end what harms us and nurture what sustains us. By contemplating Mahakali, Smashan Kali, Bhadrakali, and her many other names, we learn that true strength is not rigid. It is responsive, rooted in awareness, and guided by a love that is willing to do what is necessary for growth and balance.

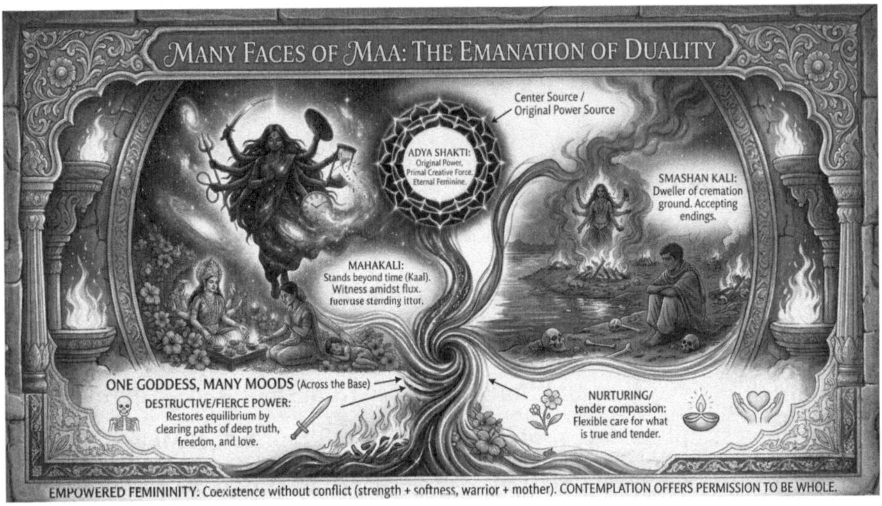

Part II - Stories of Battle and Grace

Chapter 6

BATTLES THAT SHAPE THE COSMOS: SHUMBHA AND NISHUMBHA

Among the sacred narratives of the Devi Mahatmya, the confrontation with the demon brothers Shumbha and Nishumbha reveals the goddess's supreme authority. On the surface, it is a tale of war; at a deeper level, it is a declaration of cosmic balance, where the Devi rises to shatter arrogance and restore dharma.

Shumbha and Nishumbha were no ordinary asuras. Born of insatiable ambition, they clawed their way to power through conquest and cruelty. One by one, they defeated the gods, stripped them of their celestial weapons, seized their thrones, and dimmed their radiance. Under their rule, the three worlds bent under the weight of tyranny. Convinced that no power could oppose them, the brothers proclaimed themselves lords of all existence.

Driven from their celestial homes, the gods turned in despair to the Himalayas, the ancient refuge of seekers. On snow-clad slopes, beneath endless sky and silent peaks, they gathered and raised their voices in prayer. Their hymns, filled with longing and humility, called upon the eternal Shakti, the source from which all power flows.

From that radiant stillness, the Devi manifested as Durga: calm, smiling, and resplendent, her grace masking unthinkable power. Seated upon her lion, adorned with divine weapons, she appeared not as a desperate last hope, but as a steady, sovereign presence. Her very arrival signalled that the balance of the cosmos would not be surrendered.

Soon, news of her beauty and presence reached Shumbha and Nishumbha. Intoxicated by their dominance, they saw her not as a threat, but as a prize. Shumbha sent messengers to the mountain, boasting of his wealth and empire. “All jewels, all kingdoms, all treasures of the three worlds belong to our lord,” they declared. “Let the goddess come and become his queen.”

The Devi listened and answered with a challenge that cut through their pride. She said she had vowed to marry only the one who could defeat her in battle. Her words were simple, but their meaning was clear: no authority is true if it cannot stand before truth itself. Her reply cracked the illusion that Shumbha’s rule was unquestionable.

Humiliated and enraged, Shumbha abandoned persuasion and turned to violence. His armies surged towards the mountain, darkening the earth with their sheer number. At their head marched his terrifying generals, Chanda and Munda, embodiments of brutality and bloodlust. Their weapons rang with malice, and their confidence came from long, unchallenged victory.

But the goddess did not retreat. Mounted on her lion, she met the advancing forces with a laughter that rang across the battlefield like thunder. Divine weapons flashed like lightning, and each of her movements carried both beauty and destruction. The mountains shook beneath the clash. Demon legions that once seemed invincible fell before her unrelenting force. Chanda and Munda, the symbols of crude violence, were struck down, their might reduced to nothing. As a result, the goddess came to be known by a combination of the names of the two demons: Chamundi, or Chamundeshwari.

Meanwhile, the onslaught continued. Wave after wave of demons hurled themselves at her, driven by ego and blind obedience. As the battle wore on, the Devi’s expression shifted. Her brows knit, and from her radiant forehead there spread a deep, consuming darkness, like night swallowing the sun. From that terrible and sacred threshold burst forth a new form: Maa Kali.

Her laughter tore through the skies, echoing with the end of arrogance and false power. Her form was wild, uncontainable, utterly fearless. With each step and swing of her blade, she devoured the remnants of the demon armies. Illusions crumbled before her gaze. Where Shumbha and Nishumbha had sought absolute control, Maa Kali revealed a stark truth: all domination is temporary, and all ego is ultimately devoured by time.

In this climactic moment, the story moves beyond battlefield imagery. Kali's arrival is the unveiling of the Devi's most uncompromising aspect, the force that appears when all other approaches have failed, when arrogance has grown so vast that only a complete dismantling can restore balance. To those aligned with dharma, her presence is terrifying but protective; to those clinging to adharma, she is the final boundary they cannot cross.

Through Maa Kali's fierce intervention, the tide turns. Shumbha and Nishumbha are defeated, their reign brought to an unequivocal end. The gods recover their radiance and weapons, not as trophies of revenge, but as signs that order has been re-established. The universe remembers its true alignment: not under the rule of ego, but under the guardianship of the Devi.

For a modern reader or devotee, this story can be approached on multiple levels. Outwardly, it is a divine war in which good triumphs over evil. Inwardly, Shumbha and Nishumbha can be seen as forms of inner arrogance and insecurity, the part of us that wants to control everything, that believes it is the sole centre of the universe. Their vast armies echo our many justifications, excuses, and patterns of behaviour that protect this inner tyranny.

In this light, the Devi's laughter and Kali's terrible dance are not just frightening images. They represent the moments when life, or inner truth, refuses to support our illusions any longer. A relationship collapses because it was built on pretence. A role we were proud of is taken away, revealing attachments we did not want to see. A long-avoided truth finally demands to be acknowledged. It can feel like destruction, but from a deeper perspective, something false is being removed so that something truer can stand.

The gods, stripped of their weapons and pride, symbolise another important reality: even our brightest qualities, talent, intelligence, status, spiritual knowledge, are not ultimately ours alone. They are on loan from a greater source. When we forget this and mistake borrowed brightness for personal supremacy, we fall into the very delusion that Shumbha and Nishumbha embody.

'Emergence of Kali from Durga's forehead: Devouring ego and restoring cosmic balance'

In calling upon the Devi from the Himalayas, the gods model a different stance: humility, surrender, and trust. Rather than clinging to lost power, they acknowledge their helplessness and ask for grace. It is in response to this sincerity that the Devi appears in her full strength. In our own lives, this suggests that real help often comes when we drop the mask of self-sufficiency and dare to be honest about our limitations.

Thus, the battle against Shumbha and Nishumbha is not only an episode in a sacred text, it is a recurring pattern in human experience. Whenever injustice, ego, and imbalance grow unchecked, within societies or within us, there comes a point when a Kali-like force arises to confront them. It may appear as a crisis, a confrontation, or a sudden change, but its deeper purpose is the same as in the Devi Mahatmya: to restore a more truthful order.

For devotees of Maa Kali, this story offers both warning and comfort. It warns against the subtle ways in which power and pride can take over. At the same time, it reassures us that no matter how dark the situation becomes, the mother is not absent. She may appear in a gentle form or in a fearsome one, but her intention is always rooted in protection, clarity, and ultimate liberation.

Chapter 7

BLOOD SEED AND THE DANCE OF TIME: THE TALE OF RAKTABIJA

With Shumbha and Nishumbha vanquished, the battlefield fell strangely quiet. The once-thundering armies had been reduced to ash and echoes. Broken weapons lay scattered, the dust was stained with the memory of countless clashes, and the air hung heavy with the faint smoke of fading fires. Yet even in this hard-won stillness, one last terror remained.

His name was Raktabija.

Raktabija, literally "blood seed", was no ordinary asura. His power lay in a dreadful boon: every drop of his blood that touched the earth would give rise to a new, fully formed demon, as strong as he was. Wound him, and you did not weaken him; you multiplied him.

When the battle with Raktabija began, it seemed at first like any other confrontation. Weapons were raised, mantras were invoked, and divine forces rushed to meet him. But with every blow struck against him, the ground came alive with fresh horrors. Each drop of blood that fell sprouted into another Raktabija, then another, and another. The battlefield, which had just begun to empty, was suddenly crawling with new demons, each as fierce and relentless as the first.

What should have been a final, decisive victory turned into a nightmare without end. The more the goddess and her allies fought, the more crowded the field became. Every act of resistance seemed to feed the very force they were trying to stop. The gods watched helplessly as the sky darkened with the growing swarm, and despair began to seep into their hearts.

It was in this moment of near-certain defeat that Maa Kali stepped forward. She was unafraid, fully awake to the nature of the challenge. As Goddess Durga hurled her spear and pierced Raktabija, lifting him screaming into the air, Maa Kali moved with terrifying precision. She seized him mid-flight, her eyes blazing like burning stars. Tilting her head back, she opened her mouth wide and drank.

She drank every drop of his blood, every spark of his life force, before it could touch the earth. New demons tried to form, clawing their way into existence from the spilling blood, only to be swallowed instantly. Raktabija thrashed and howled, but there was no escape. The very boon he had relied upon now betrayed him. What once made him invincible became the pathway to his end. With the last drop consumed, the demon was destroyed.

Victory, however, brought with it a new danger. The fury awakened in Maa Kali during the battle did not subside when Raktabija fell. Her blood was still aflame with the intensity of destruction. She began the tandava, the dance of destruction. With each step, the earth trembled. With each movement, it seemed as though the very fabric of the cosmos might tear. What had started as a battle against one asura now threatened to become a force that could undo worlds.

The gods, who had just been rescued from despair, found themselves afraid once more, this time, of the very power that had saved them. Seeing this, they turned to Lord Shiva. Calm where all else was chaos, he chose a path of profound humility. He lay down silently on the ground, in the path of Maa Kali's dance.

Lost in her frenzy, Kali stepped upon him. In that single instant, contact with Shiva, her own consort, pure consciousness itself, brought her back to awareness. She realised where she stood, and on whom. Shock and shame surged through her. She bit her tongue, her expression changing from raging fury to sudden stillness. With that pause, the dance that had threatened to end all worlds came to a halt.

This moment became an eternal image: Maa Kali standing with one foot on Shiva's chest, her tongue extended, her eyes wide with the recognition of what she has almost done. It is perhaps one of the most iconic depictions of the goddess, a snapshot of power meeting awareness, of unstoppable force tempered by consciousness.

The tale of Raktabija can be read as dramatic mythology, but also as a layered teaching.

Raktabija represents patterns that grow stronger the more we fight them blindly. Certain fears, obsessions, or habits behave like "blood seeds": each time we attack them without understanding, they seem to multiply. Anger answered only with more anger, for instance, often expands conflict. Shame that is pushed down instead of faced can return in many forms. In this sense, Raktabija is not only a demon on a battlefield; he is a symbol of the problems that feed on our unexamined reactions.

Maa Kali's way of dealing with him is radical. She does not simply strike harder; she changes the entire strategy. Instead of letting his blood spill and multiply, she absorbs it completely. Symbolically, this is the act of total, fearless confrontation. Rather than pushing away what is dark or painful, she takes it into herself, transforms it, and denies it the chance to replicate. It is a fierce, uncompromising mercy.

Her wild tandava after the victory is another reminder that immense power, even when used for protection, must be held in awareness. Shiva lying down in her path shows that pure consciousness does not resist her but offers itself as a grounding presence. When Kali's foot touches Shiva, destruction meets stillness, and a new balance is born. For us, this suggests that courage and clarity must work together. Energy without awareness can become chaos; awareness without energy can remain distant and inactive.

In everyday life, the story of Raktabija invites us to look at what in us behaves like "blood seed," and where a Kali-like approach might be needed. Some patterns cannot be managed with half-measures. They require full attention, honest acknowledgement, and the willingness to stop feeding them in the old ways. At the same time, the story also reminds us to temper our inner tandava with the quiet presence of Shiva, an inner stillness that keeps even our fiercest transformations aligned with wisdom.

Through this tale, Maa Kali appears once again not only as a destroyer of outer demons, but as a profound guide for inner change. She shows that certain cycles of suffering must be ended at the root, and that true endings, however intense, are in service of a deeper, more enduring peace.

Chapter 8

FROM SILENCE TO SONG: KALIDASA AND MAA KALI'S GRACE

Not all of Maa Kali's stories unfold on cosmic battlefields. Some take place in quiet courtyards, royal halls, and dimly lit temples within the very ordinary spaces of human life. The tale of Kalidasa, one of India's greatest poets and playwrights, is one such story. Here, the goddess does not wield a sword. She transforms a life from the inside.

According to tradition, Kalidasa did not begin his life as a celebrated poet. He was, by most accounts, a man of striking simplicity. He had little formal education, no reputation for cleverness, and none of the refinement prized in royal courts. Words did not come easily to him. In a world that honoured debate and scholarship, he lived quietly on the margins, performing humble tasks and remaining largely unnoticed.

In the same kingdom lived princess Vidyottama, famed for her sharp intellect and formidable pride. Learned and articulate, she announced that she would marry only a man capable of defeating her in philosophical argument. Scholar after scholar was invited, and one by one they were defeated, their arguments dismantled, their confidence wounded. Humiliated, some of these scholars turned not towards deeper learning, but towards resentment.

In their bitterness, they plotted a cruel trick. They dressed the simple Kalidasa in fine robes, adorned him like a great thinker, and presented him before the princess as a silent sage. His quietness was misread as depth, his hesitation as subtle wisdom. Impressed or perhaps challenged by the mystery, Vidyottama married him.

The illusion did not last long. Once within the privacy of marriage, the princess discovered the truth. Her husband could barely read. He could not debate. He did not understand the philosophies she cherished or the scriptures she had mastered. Shock turned to anger, anger to shame. Feeling deceived and humiliated, she lashed out at Kalidasa.

In some versions of the story, it is said that she commanded him to go to the temple of Maa Kali, to pray with full devotion, and to bolt the door from within. Whether out of obedience, despair, or a mixture of both, Kalidasa went.

Inside the temple, the atmosphere was different from the world that had judged him. Lamps flickered, casting moving shadows on the stone floor. The scent of incense and flowers lingered in the air. Before him stood the image of Maa Kali: dark, fierce, yet strangely intimate. Kalidasa had no complex mantras to offer, no polished hymns, no philosophical insights. He had only his raw, unpolished heart.

So, he prayed with that.

He bowed down and poured out his pain: the humiliation of being mocked, the confusion of being trapped in a life he did not understand, the weight of his wife's anger, the ache of feeling small and inadequate in a world that worshipped brilliance. He did not try to impress the goddess with clever words. Instead, he surrendered his ego, his pretences, and his helplessness at her feet.

Moved by the sincerity of his devotion, Maa Kali is said to have appeared before him. In her presence, ignorance was not scolded; it was burned away. She granted him gifts that seemed impossible for a man of his background: wisdom, sensitivity, command of language, and the power to shape thought into poetry.

Where once his mind had been silent and hesitant, it now flowed with metaphor, rhythm, and insight, as if a river long dammed had been suddenly set free.

When Kalidasa emerged from the temple, he was no longer the same man. The world outside had not changed. The court, the expectations, the memories of deception were all still there but something fundamental within him had shifted. He carried a new clarity, a new depth.

According to the tale, when princess Vidyottama saw him again, she tested him. "Asti kaścid vāgviśeṣaḥ?" she asked, "Have you acquired any special power of speech that would make me welcome you differently?" His answer was not a single line or clever comeback. Instead, he composed great works of literature, beginning each with one of those three words she had spoken. In time, these works would be counted among the finest in Sanskrit.

His name itself is believed to reflect his transformation: Kali-dasa, the servant of Kali. He was a servant not in the sense of passive submission, but in devotion, gratitude, and creative offering. His genius was not claimed as private property. It was understood as grace, shakti flowing through a vessel that had been emptied of ego and filled with faith.

This tale offers a different kind of teaching about Maa Kali. In the stories of cosmic battle, she destroys asuras and restores balance in the three worlds. Here, she destroys a more intimate kind of ignorance; The belief that someone is fixed, limited, or permanently "less than" because of their beginnings. She awakens the potential hidden in an apparently ordinary soul.

For readers and devotees, the story of Kalidasa speaks to several truths. It reminds us that intellectual pride, however sophisticated, can be blind. The princess, for all her brilliance, could not imagine that someone like Kalidasa could ever stand beside her as an equal. Yet, it is through the grace of the goddess that he surpasses the expectations of everyone who underestimated him. At the same time, the story is not a celebration of cleverness alone. Kalidasa's transformation does not come from argument; it comes from surrender. In a modern world that often values performance over sincerity, the tale suggests that real growth begins not with showing off what we know, but with admitting what we don't. Maa Kali does not reward arrogance disguised as knowledge. She responds to honesty, vulnerability, and a heart willing to bow down without pretence.

This story also offers comfort to those who feel unseen or underestimated. It says that our starting point does not define our ending. The labels placed upon us by family, society, or circumstance are not the final truth. There is always more within us than what the world has measured. When we turn sincerely towards the divine, towards truth, towards inner transformation, new capacities can emerge, often in ways we could never have predicted.

Through Kalidasa, Maa Kali appears as an awakener of dormant brilliance, the one who can transform a life not by changing its outer setting first, but by igniting its inner light. In her presence, even the most overlooked person can become a channel for beauty, wisdom, and meaning. And in recognising this, we are invited to look at ourselves and others with softer, more patient eyes, remembering that anyone, at any moment, might be standing on the threshold of their own temple, waiting for a grace that could change everything.

PART III - LIVING TRADITIONS

Chapter 9

A MOTHER WHO LISTENS: BHAKTI TRADITIONS

If folk traditions present Maa Kali as the village guardian, and tantric paths seek her in cremation grounds and inner disciplines, bhakti traditions bring her into the most intimate space of all: the human heart. In bhakti, she is not primarily approached as a distant cosmic force, but as a mother who can be loved, argued with, pleaded with, and trusted.

A defining feature of Kali bhakti is the transformation of fear into love. Many devotees describe their journey with her as beginning in awe, or even terror struck by her fearsome iconography, and slowly deepening into trust and affection. Over time, her wild hair and fierce expression are no longer seen as signs of cruelty, but as a protective ferocity, like a mother who will go to any length to defend her children. In this emotional shift lies the heart of Bengali Kali devotion.

In bhakti, Maa Kali is not a distant queen or abstract principle. She is "Kali Maa," a living presence who listens and responds. Devotees speak to her freely, sometimes affectionately, sometimes with frustration, confident that she can absorb all their emotions. She is the one they turn to before exams, during illness, after failures, and in moments of joy. The relationship is personal and exclusive: she is their Maa, and they are her child.

SONGS OF LONGING: RAMPRASAD SEN

One of the most influential voices in Kali bhakti is the 18th-century poet Ramprasad Sen. His songs, known as Shyama Sangeet, helped transform Kali from a fearsome goddess of cremation grounds into an emotionally accessible mother for ordinary householders.

Ramprasad did not address Maa Kali with ritual distance. In his songs, he complains that she ignores him, begs for her protection, questions her silence, and ultimately surrenders to her will. He speaks to her as a stubborn, loving son might speak to his mother, sometimes scolding, sometimes weeping, sometimes laughing, always trusting that she will understand the depth beneath his words.

Through Ramprasad's poetry, Kali became someone with whom devotees could have a real conversation. People who would never perform tantric sadhana in a cremation ground could now sit at home, sing his songs, and feel close to her. The goddess who once seemed terrifying now appeared as a playful, unpredictable, deeply loving mother who might test her children, but never abandon them.

A MOTHER IN THE HOME: EVERYDAY KALI BHAKTI

In many Bengali households, bhakti to Maa Kali is woven into daily life. A small image or shrine may stand in a corner of the home. Before important events like a child's exam, a journey, or a surgery, family members pause to bow their heads and speak to her. Mothers often play a central role: they teach children to say "Jai Maa" when afraid, to tell her their worries, and to trust her care.

Devotion is not limited to formal rituals. It appears in simple acts: lighting a lamp at dusk, offering a few flowers, whispering her name in the quiet moments between tasks. For many, she becomes the silent listener to their private fears and secret hopes. The relationship is not always calm; devotees may complain to her, question her decisions, or tell her bluntly that they feel neglected. Yet beneath all this lies an unshakeable assumption: Maa knows best.

Kali Puja, celebrated especially on the new moon night of Diwali in Bengal, brings this intimacy into a wider community space. Entire neighbourhoods organise pujas with decorated altars, lights, music, and offerings. Lamps glow in the deep darkness, symbolising her presence amid chaos and uncertainty. Families stay awake through the night, singing hymns, telling stories, and sharing prasad. Compared to the grand public spectacle of Durga Puja, Kali Puja often has a more concentrated, devotional atmosphere, less focussed on display, more on direct connection with the goddess.

RAMAKRISHNA AT DAKSHINESHWAR: LOVE AS WORSHIP

Among the most famous examples of Kali bhakti in practice is Sri Ramakrishna Paramahamsa, the 19th-century mystic of Dakshineshwar Kali Temple near Kolkata. As a temple priest, he did not treat the image of Kali as a symbol alone. For him, she was a living mother.

Ramakrishna spoke to Maa Kali, wept for her vision, and often entered states of intense spiritual emotion, or bhava, in her presence. At times he would complain to her like a child, at others he would lose all sense of separation, seeing her as both form and formlessness, the loving mother and the infinite consciousness behind all religions.

His devotion blended bhakti with tantric experience and Vedantic insight, but at its core was a childlike love and total dependence. Dakshineshwar became, and remains, a pilgrimage site where devotees seek Maa Kali's grace not primarily through harsh austerities, but through prayer, song, and surrender.

TRUSTING MAA THROUGH SUFFERING

A key theme in Kali bhakti is total dependence on the goddess, even when life is painful. Devotees often say, "Maa knows best," not as a cliché, but as a lived attitude. Hardship is interpreted as part of her mysterious way of shaping and strengthening her children.

Stories circulate, sometimes recorded, sometimes passed down orally of devotees who lost wealth, health, or even family members, yet remained deeply devoted to Maa Kali. They believed that, in ways they could not yet understand, her hidden compassion would ultimately lead them towards liberation or inner peace. This trust does not deny grief; it places grief in a larger context of relationship with the divine.

In this way, Kali bhakti offers emotional resilience. It allows people to endure uncertainty and loss without losing meaning. Maa Kali is not expected to prevent all suffering. Instead, she is believed to walk with her devotees through it, sometimes silently, sometimes with unmistakable signs. She becomes the one constant presence in a life full of changes.

FROM FEAR TO INTIMACY

Through bhakti, Maa Kali's image transforms. She is no longer only the fierce goddess of cremation grounds or blood sacrifice; she becomes the mother whose terrifying appearance hides boundless compassion. Her garland of heads and wild hair no longer push the devotee away. They become familiar, even beloved, features of someone deeply known.

This transformation from fear to intimacy is central to understanding her place in the devotional heart of Bengal and beyond. It shows that the same goddess who stands on battlefields and in Smashan can also sit quietly in the corner of a small home, listening to a child's whispered prayer.

In the next chapters, as we turn to folk and tantric traditions, this bhakti lens will remain in the background. Whether she appears as a village guardian, a cremation-ground guide, or an inner force of kundalini, the mother who listens and loves is never far away.

Chapter 10

THE VILLAGE GUARDIAN: FOLK TRADITIONS

In countless villages across India, Maa Kali is not a distant cosmic abstraction. She is the immediate guardian of the community, woven into the daily rhythms of rural life. She dwells in stones, trees, riverbanks, and cremation grounds, recognised less through texts and more through lived experience.

In folk Shaktism, each village may know her differently. The Kali of one place is never assumed to be identical to the Kali of another. In one village she may protect cattle, in another she may guard women in childbirth, in yet another she may be the one who wards off epidemics and famine. These local forms of the goddess function as gramadevata, territorial guardians whose power is effective precisely because it is rooted in that particular land and community.

STONES THAT BECOME GODDESSES

Many village shrines to Maa Kali are born not from planned temple projects, but from encounters and dreams. A common pattern is the dream-command, or svapnadesha, in which the goddess appears to a devotee and asks to be brought into the social world. Often, such dreams lead to the discovery of a black, rounded stone in a pond, riverbed, or field.

Once found, the stone is not immediately placed in a grand temple. It may first be set under a tree, fed with offerings, and smeared with vermilion. Over time, as more people come, offer prayers, and experience her presence, the simple spot evolves. A thatched shelter is built, later replaced by brick walls, and eventually, the site may grow into a known pilgrimage place. In this upwards movement from fieldstone to temple, the belief shines through that the goddess gains power and social presence not through texts alone, but through attention, offerings, and relationship.

At Makardah village in Howrah, for example, the goddess is worshipped in the form of a stone said to have changed size over time. Oral traditions recall that it was once so large the priest needed a ladder to perform daily worship. Tired and overwhelmed, he complained about the burden of caring for such a massive deity. In response, the goddess is said to have withdrawn into the earth. Only when the community repented did she reappear, smaller and more manageable. The story carries a simple but striking message: the goddess responds emotionally to human attitudes and respect.

ANCESTRESS AND OLD WOMAN: BUDI MA

Among Adivasi and folk Hindu communities, Maa Kali often appears in the form of Budi Ma, the Old Woman or ancestress. Unlike the youthful, fierce images of classical iconography, Budi Ma derives her authority from age and origin. She is honoured outdoors, under trees or near stones, without the elaborate sculptures or decorations found in large temples.

In Tentulhiti village in Purulia, the annual Jatra Budi festival also known as Bhadu Puja, honours such an ancestral goddess beneath a sal tree. Offerings of rice, bangles, sweets, and animals are made. The rituals include a dramatic communal act in which sacrificial animals are torn apart and shared among the villagers. Rather than being seen as senseless violence, this act is explained as a lesson in restraint and collective responsibility: no one may hoard more than they can physically hold. The ritual thus becomes a teaching on sharing and social ethics, expressed through intense, embodied symbolism.

Another example comes from Asansol, near Burdwan, where a goddess later known as Ghaghrabudi was revealed after a flood exposed certain stones. Over time, as Hindu worshippers adopted and interpreted her, she became Ghaghradevi, blending folk Kali traditions with broader Hindu frameworks without erasing her local origins. Here again, we see Maa taking root in a specific geography and community story.

OFFERINGS, SACRIFICE, AND RECIPROCITY

In folk contexts, devotion to Maa Kali is direct and embodied. Offerings often include flowers and food but can also involve animal sacrifice, especially goats and fowl, as acts of reciprocal nourishment. The goddess is fed so that she, in turn, will feed and protect her people.

Historical accounts mention that, in earlier periods, even human blood offerings were reported in respectable households, with small amounts taken from the chest and offered to Kali during times of crisis. Within these communities, such acts were not perceived as cruelty, but as intense forms of protective exchange. A fed goddess protects, a neglected goddess may retaliate. Her ferocity is not denied, it is honoured and consciously engaged with.

Maa Kali, in this vision, is not a soft, passive presence in the background. She is the ultimate defender against disease, infertility, premature death, and misfortune. People do not approach her asking for mild blessings alone. They come to her when the stakes are high.

FESTIVALS, POSSESSION, AND WOMEN'S VOICES

Village festivals bring Kali's presence into collective experience. During these celebrations, possession is a central religious phenomenon, especially among women. Trance mediums, often women from ordinary social backgrounds, begin to shake, speak, and move in ways that the community recognises as the goddess entering them.

In these moments, Maa Kali is no longer distant or symbolic. She is audible, embodied, and socially active. Through the possessed medium, she may diagnose illnesses, demand specific offerings, bless, warn, or heal devotees. Her words carry authority, sometimes more than that of formal priests or local leaders.

Such possession grants religious power to women who might otherwise be marginalised in everyday hierarchies. When they speak in Kali's voice, people listen. The goddess thus becomes a channel through which suppressed voices can emerge and be honoured, even within traditional structures.

A GODDESS WHO BELONGS TO HER PEOPLE

Across these varied folk forms, stones discovered by dreams, Budi Ma under a tree, goddesses emerging from flood-exposed rocks, trance-speaking mediums, the same pattern repeats: Maa Kali is deeply local, specific, and relational. She does not belong only to grand temples or Sanskrit verses. She belongs to fields, villages, riverbanks, and family histories.

Rather than a universal abstraction, she becomes "our goddess" tied to particular soil, particular stories, and particular needs. For the villagers who worship her, she is not one option among many divine forms. She is the one who has chosen them and their land, and to whom they, in turn, give their loyalty, offerings, and trust.

In the next chapter, as we step from village shrines into cremation grounds and inner practices, this sense of immediacy will remain. Whether as a stone under a tree or as a presence in the depths of meditation, Maa Kali continues to meet her devotees exactly where they are.

Chapter 11

FIRE IN THE CREMATION GROUND: TANTRIC TRADITIONS

While folk traditions place Maa Kali in the intimate spaces of village life, tantric traditions seek her in more unsettling landscapes such as cremation grounds, forests, and the hidden interior of the human body. In tantric Shaktism, she is not only a protector but a source of transformative knowledge, power, and liberation.

Tantric paths do not aim to make life more comfortable. They turn deliberately towards what most people avoid: death, fear, impurity, and the unknown. In this confrontation, Maa Kali appears as the one who can guide a seeker through terror into freedom.

SMASHAN: THE CREMATION GROUND AS TEMPLE

One of the most emblematic settings of tantric Kali worship is the cremation ground, or Smashan. Here, social order and ideas of purity fall away. The body, which we usually carefully protect and decorate, is reduced to ash. All human roles such as parent, child, leader, outcast become equal before the fire.

Tantrikas choose this environment deliberately. By meditating among funeral pyres, bones, and wandering spirits, they confront the two fears that shape much of human behaviour: fear of death and fear of losing control. Maa

Kali, who stands upon Shiva's body and wears a garland of skulls, is believed to reveal herself most readily where death is fully present.

At Tarapith in Bengal, one of the most famous Shakta sites, Maa Kali is worshipped alongside the cremation ground itself. Tantric practitioners traditionally performed their sadhana there at night, sitting on the edge of the burning ghat. Their goal was not to perform spectacle, but to remain calm, focused, and inwardly steady amid sights and sounds that would terrify most people. In doing so, they sought to prove their readiness for the goddess's direct, uncompromising grace.

AWAKENING THE INNER KALI: KUNDALINI SHAKTI

Unlike folk worship, which emphasises external offerings, tantric traditions often turn the focus inward. In kundalini yoga, widely practised by Shakta tantrikas in Bengal, Maa Kali is identified with Kundalini Shakti, the coiled serpent energy said to rest at the base of the spine.

Through mantra, breath control, visualisation, and disciplined meditation, the practitioner works to awaken this inner goddess and guide her upward through the chakras to unite with Shiva at the crown of the head. As this inner ascent unfolds, seekers describe intense physical and psychological experiences: heat rising in the body, trembling, spontaneous movements, visions of light, and states of overwhelming bliss or, at times, terror.

These phenomena are interpreted not as illness, but as signs of Maa Kali's awakening power, where she becomes the force animating consciousness itself. In this view, Kali is no longer only an external deity; she is the deep, vibrating energy at the core of one's own being.

SKULLS, ASHES, AND THE BREAKING OF TABOO

Tantric Kali worship often uses symbols that appear extreme: skulls, bones, ashes, and occasionally blood. The purpose is not to glorify violence, but to deliberately shatter the conventional boundaries of purity and impurity that keep people trapped in fear and social conditioning.

A tantrika may sit on a seat of five skulls, known as the panchamunda asana. This posture symbolises mastery over the fear of death and the limitations of the ego. By placing his or her practice literally on the reminders of mortality, the seeker is forced to confront the truth that all forms, including one's own identity, are temporary.

One striking modern example is Prahlad Chandra Brahmachari, a Kali devotee and tantric practitioner from Ramnathpur. Though illiterate and lacking formal training, he was said to be guided by Kali through dreams and visions. He meditated at cremation grounds, offered his own blood to the goddess on new-moon nights, and sat above buried skulls in his meditation hut. To his devotees, these acts were not seen as theatrics, but as evidence of Kali's direct intervention and his transformation into her instrument.

YOGINIS AND DIRECT INITIATION

Tantric traditions also speak of yoginis, female beings who inhabit forests, cremation grounds, and subtle realms. In folk tantra, yoginis may appear as supernatural women who grant wealth, protection, or knowledge, but demand exclusive devotion in return. In classical tantra, they are interpreted more symbolically as forces of consciousness or guardians of specific forms of wisdom.

A key element that distinguishes tantric practice from more orthodox paths is the belief that initiation can come directly from the goddess, not only from a human guru. Many practitioners are said to have received mantras, ritual instructions, or yogic techniques through dreams or visions of Kali herself. This prophetic call resembles the dream-commands of folk traditions but is oriented towards intense personal sadhana rather than village welfare.

In this way, tantric Kali worship survives less through large institutions and more through secrecy, lineage, and lived experience. It is kept alive in private rituals, hidden meditation huts, and in the inner journeys of practitioners who continue to face her terrifying grace.

DESTROYER AND LIBERATOR

Through the tantric lens, Maa Kali appears as both destroyer and liberator. She strips away fear, ego, and the layers of social conditioning that keep a person bound. The methods may seem extreme, but their aim is radical freedom.

For most readers, a life of Smashan sadhana and skull-seats may not be the path. Yet the inner logic of tantric Kali practice carries a universal message: true transformation often requires us to face what we fear most, rather than endlessly trying to stay comfortable. Skulls and ashes may be outward symbols, but they point inward to the courage to acknowledge our own mortality, limitations, and attachments, and to discover that beneath all of them, a deeper, freer self is waiting.

In the final chapters, as we turn to Maa Kali's contemporary significance and her teachings for modern life, this tantric understanding will sit alongside bhakti warmth and folk intimacy. Together, they reveal a goddess who meets us in every layer of existence, from the village path to the cremation ground, from temple ritual to the quiet centre of our own awareness.

Part IV - Kali and Our Inner Lives

Chapter 12

KALI IN OUR TIMES: COURAGE, TRUTH, AND INNER CHANGE

While rituals and traditions offer sacred ways to connect with Maa Kali, her significance reaches far beyond temple walls and festival nights. Her symbols and stories carry deep meaning for contemporary life, speaking to people across belief systems, identities, and experiences. In a world shaped by performance, pressure, and appearances, her presence invites us back to what is real, essential, and transformative.

We live in an age dominated by social media trends and constant visibility. Sameness is often rewarded, while individuality is quietly discouraged. There is pressure to fit into narrow templates of success, beauty, productivity, and even spirituality. In such an environment, authenticity can feel risky.

Maa Kali stands in direct opposition to this culture of imitation. She is unapologetically herself, raw, uncontained, and unconcerned with external approval. Her wild hair, unadorned form, and fearless stance reject imposed standards and artificial refinement. Through her, we are reminded that authenticity is not rebellion for its own sake, it is an act of truth. She teaches us to live honestly, to honour our inner voice, and to resist the urge to dilute ourselves simply to be accepted.

Imagine a young professional who feels compelled to curate every aspect of their life for others' approval, filtering photos, editing opinions, hiding vulnerability. Remembering Kali's presence, they begin, slowly, to show up a little more honestly: saying "no" where they once always said "yes," admitting when they are tired, expressing opinions without first measuring them against trends. These may seem like small acts, but in a world of masks, such honesty is deeply sacred.

COURAGE TO FACE DARKNESS

This commitment to authenticity is inseparable from Maa Kali's symbolism of courage. She does not look away from darkness, but steps into it. On battlefields, in cremation grounds, and in the hidden corners of the heart, she represents the strength required to face what we fear rather than endlessly avoiding it.

In modern life, this courage often takes quieter forms. It might look like acknowledging long-suppressed pain, seeking help for mental health struggles, leaving a harmful situation, standing up against injustice at personal cost, or choosing integrity over comfort. Maa Kali's raised sword is not only a weapon of destruction; it is the clarity that cuts through denial and falsehood. She reminds us that courage is not the absence of fear, but the willingness to act despite it.

Consider someone who has spent years avoiding a difficult conversation with a family member, fearing conflict. When they finally sit down, speak honestly, and listen in return, the outcome may not be perfect but something heavy shifts. Silence and resentment begin to lose their grip. In that moment of trembling honesty, something of Kali's sword has moved.

TRANSFORMATION THROUGH ENDINGS

At a deeper level, Maa Kali embodies inner transformation. As the goddess of time and dissolution, she governs endings as much as beginnings. Her garland of skulls and her dance upon the battlefield symbolise the death of ego, attachment, and illusion. To stand under her gaze is to know that certain things in us cannot be gently reshaped, they must be let go.

In contemporary terms, this speaks to the necessity of releasing identities, beliefs, and emotional patterns that no longer serve us. We may cling to roles we have outgrown, opinions inherited rather than examined, or habits rooted in fear or pride. Transformation, as Maa Kali teaches, is rarely gentle. It can be unsettling and uncomfortable. Yet it is through this inner "destruction" that genuine growth and renewal become possible, and in doing so, she frees the self.

A person who has always defined themselves only by career success, for example, may face a sudden job loss. At first, this feels like pure devastation. Over time, with reflection and support, they begin to discover parts of themselves that were buried under constant striving, in the form of creativity, relationships, spiritual curiosity. Though painful, the ending becomes a turning point. In hindsight, they may see Maa Kali's hand in the collapse of what was never meant to be the whole of their identity.

STRENGTH AND COMPASSION TOGETHER

One of Maa Kali's most powerful teachings for our time lies in her balance of strength and compassion. She is fierce without being cruel, protective without being passive. Her maternal love does not appear as indulgence, but as a firm guardianship of truth and justice.

In a world that often frames strength and compassion as opposites, Kali reveals their deep interdependence. True compassion sometimes requires firmness: setting boundaries, saying difficult truths, refusing to enable harm. True strength, when rooted in awareness, is never devoid of care. This balance is especially relevant in leadership, relationships, parenting, and self-growth, where the challenge lies in being both assertive and humane.

We might think of a parent who must say “no” to something a child desperately wants, not out of control, but out of love and foresight. Or a leader who refuses to tolerate unethical behaviour, even when it is popular or profitable. In such moments, softness alone is not enough; nor is hardness. What is needed is Kali’s blend of sharp clarity and deep concern.

EXPANSIVE FEMININITY AND HUMAN WHOLENESS

Maa Kali’s representation of femininity challenges narrow, restrictive ideals. She refuses to be confined to gentleness, beauty, or pleasing behaviour. She is ambition, rage, protection, tenderness, and liberation all at once. By her very presence, she challenges social structures that restrict how women, and by extension, all individuals are permitted to exist and express themselves. Her femininity is expansive and sovereign. It suggests that wholeness comes not from compressing ourselves into safe, acceptable shapes, but from embracing our full complexity. For women, this can mean allowing anger to be acknowledged alongside love, strength to stand beside vulnerability, and freedom to coexist with responsibility. For men and people of all genders, Kali opens a path to a more honest humanity, where certain emotions and qualities are no longer forbidden by rigid expectations.

WALKING WITH MAA IN MODERN LIFE

Ultimately, Maa Kali is a limitless divine force, far beyond complete human comprehension. Yet her symbolism continues to offer guidance as we navigate the complexities of modern existence. She urges us to be authentic in a world of imitation, courageous in the face of fear, willing to transform rather than cling, and capable of holding strength and compassion in equal measure.

Engaging with her does not necessarily require elaborate rituals. It can begin with small, sincere gestures: sitting quietly before her image, reflecting on what needs to end and what wants to begin, asking for the courage to speak the truth, or simply saying, “Maa, show me where I am hiding from myself.” In this sense, every honest moment becomes a kind of Kali sadhana.

As the poet and devotee Ramprasad Sen expressed so beautifully in the bhakti tradition, to enter her depths is to encounter unexpected riches. To turn towards Maa Kali is not to surrender to chaos, but to truth, and in that surrender lies a freedom more profound than the safety we once tried to preserve.

Chapter 13

SITTING WITH MAA: REFLECTIONS AND REMEMBERING

By now, we have met Maa Kali in many forms, on battlefields and in cremation grounds, in village shrines and household altars, in songs of longing and in the quiet of inner transformation. We have seen her as destroyer and mother, as time and tenderness, as fierce protector and intimate guide.

And yet, no number of chapters can fully contain her. Maa Kali is, by her very nature, larger than any single image, story, or idea. The purpose of this book has not been to "explain" her completely, but to open a doorway. The rest of the journey is personal.

A MOMENT TO PAUSE

Maa Kali does not ask for perfection.

She asks for honesty.

Perhaps, this is also a space to sit with a few questions.

- Where in my life am I still hiding behind illusion or fear?
- What is asking to end, so that something truer can begin?
- What part of me needs Kali's courage to speak or act differently?
- Where am I trying too hard to control what must be surrendered to time?

- How can I bring more honesty and compassion together in one place, like her strength and her love?

You do not need immediate answers, only the willingness to see yourself clearly.

THE ULTIMATE SURRENDER

In the Kali tradition, the deepest movement is not towards control, but towards surrender.

Not as withdrawal from life, but as a quiet recognition that we are not the sole doers of all that unfolds.

A well-known line by Sri Ramakrishna Paramahamsa expresses this:

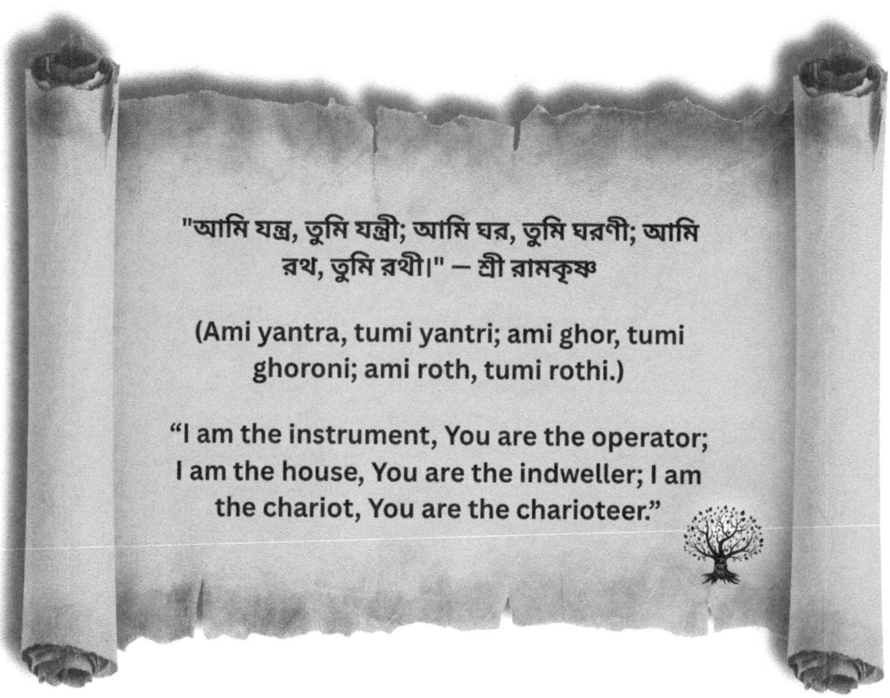

As these pages come to a close, nothing truly ends.

Maa Kali does not remain within stories or symbols.

She is there—
in what changes,
in what falls away,
and in what quietly asks to be seen.

And perhaps, in moments when everything feels uncertain, there is still something that does not turn away.

Jai Maa Kali

APPENDIX

THE DASA MAHAVIDYAS: THE TEN WISDOM FORMS OF THE DIVINE MOTHER

In the Shakta tradition, the Divine Mother is also understood through the ten Mahavidyas, ten forms that reveal different aspects of existence. Together, they represent the full spectrum of life, from creation and beauty to loss, transformation, and inner awakening.

According to tradition, there came a moment when Lord Shiva and Sati did not agree. As Shiva moved away, Sati revealed herself in ten powerful forms, appearing in every direction and surrounding him completely. Through this, she revealed that she is not limited to a single form, but is the entire power of existence, present everywhere.

Together, these ten forms came to be known as the Mahavidyas.

THE TEN FACES OF WISDOM: AN OVERVIEW

To understand the Mahavidyas, think of each goddess as a unique frequency of energy or a different chapter in the cycle of life.

KALI: THE POWER OF TIME

She is the raw, untamed force of transformation. Kali dissolves what is stagnant and "old" to create space for the new, teaching us that endings are not just inevitable, but necessary for growth.

TARA: THE ULTIMATE LIFELINE

She is the guiding light in life's most turbulent storms. When the path ahead is obscured by chaos or fear, Tara acts as the "Star" that steers you to safety, offering a fierce yet protective energy that ensures you cross over any obstacle.

TRIPURA SUNDARI: THE JOY IN THE MOMENT

She is the energy of total fulfillment and divine perfection. Beyond mere outward appearance, she represents the soul's highest state of contentment; the sovereign power that proves life is not just a struggle to be endured, but a masterpiece to be enjoyed.

BHUVANESHWARI: THE ULTIMATE HOME

She is the infinite container of all existence. Beyond just physical location, she represents the fundamental structure of reality; the sovereign power that provides the foundation for everything to exist. She teaches us that we are always supported by the vastness of the universe.

BHAIRAVI: THE ENERGY OF DETERMINATION

She is the intense heat of the inner forge. Bhairavi represents the fierce concentration and mental fire required to burn away distractions and impurities. She is the power of the "grind," the unwavering resolve that refuses to quit until the goal is achieved.

CHHINNAMASTA: THE ULTIMATE REALITY CHECK

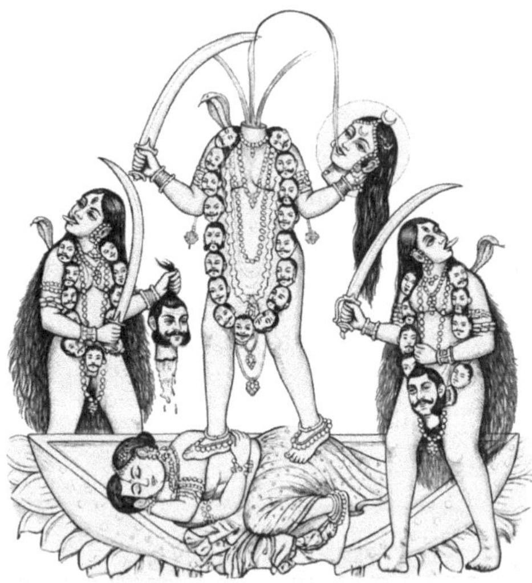

She represents the paradox of life: that we must "lose our heads" to find our souls. Chhinnamasta is the lightning strike of awareness that stops the mind's endless chatter. She teaches us that true wisdom is self-sustaining and that the greatest sacrifice is letting go of the false identity we've built for ourselves.

DHUMAVATI: THE SOUL'S QUIET TIME

She is the strength found in the "aftermath." Beyond the initial sting of loss, Dhumavati represents the indestructible wisdom that remains when everything else has fallen away. She teaches us that even in our darkest or loneliest moments, there is a resilient power that cannot be destroyed.

BAGALAMUKHI: THE POWER OF THE MUTE BUTTON

She is the power of the "Freeze." Bagalamukhi doesn't just fight; she neutralizes conflict by stopping it in its tracks. She represents the ultimate command over your own reactions; the fierce authority required to paralyze a destructive impulse or silence a toxic situation before it can escalate.

MATANGI: YOUR CREATIVE EDGE

She is the raw energy behind every word spoken and every note played. Matangi represents the mastery of communication; the fierce ability to turn your inner thoughts into a masterpiece. She is the force that allows you to speak your truth with absolute conviction, regardless of what the world thinks.

KAMALA: THE ENERGY OF GRATITUDE

She is the energy of total prosperity, not just in the bank, but in the spirit. Kamala represents the state of being "enough" and having enough. She is the sovereign power that attracts success, luxury, and the resources needed to build a legacy that lasts for generations.

WHY SEEK THE TEN WISDOMS?

Most people turn to these goddesses to dissolve fear and cultivate a deeper kind of wisdom. For the everyday seeker, the message is simple: no part of life is "bad" or beyond the reach of the divine. Whether you are basking in success (Kamala), feeling the glow of love (Sundari), or navigating the quiet shadows of a rough patch (Dhumavati), the Divine Mother is right there. She doesn't just watch over your life; she is the energy within every chapter of your story.

ACKNOWLEDGEMENT

I bow in deep reverence to Maa Kali, the eternal force of transformation and the embodiment of the infinite, whose divine presence inspired every word of Ananta The Infinite Journey of Maa Kali. This book is not merely written, it is offered at Her lotus feet with devotion and surrender.

I extend my heartfelt gratitude to my family, my parents, Dr. Pratap Mukherjee and Mrs. Jhimli Mukherjee, and my friends, whose unwavering love, strength, and encouragement have been my constant support. Their faith in me has been a guiding light throughout this journey.

I am sincerely thankful to the entire team at RidhzWorld Publishing for guiding me along this purposeful and enriching path. Your encouragement, insights, and belief in this work have played a significant role in bringing this book to life. A special note of gratitude to Chitra Divgi for her thoughtful and meticulous editing.

Lastly, I offer my deepest appreciation to all spiritual seekers whose quest for truth and higher understanding continues to inspire this journey. It is for you that these pages have been written, with the hope that Maa Kali's divine energy illuminates your path, just as She has illuminated mine.

With deepest gratitude

Pragati Mukherjee